Table of Contents
Spelling Homework Booklet
Grade 1

Start the Race!

Letter Bank

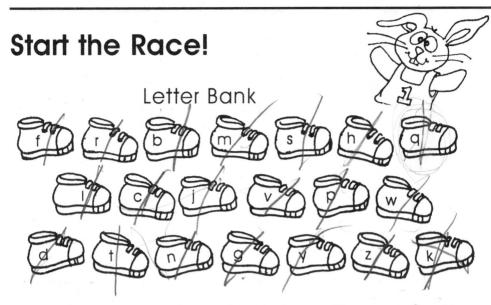

Say the name of each picture. Then write the letter that makes the beginning sound.

__h__ and

__y__ arn

__n__ est

__M__ at

__d__ og

__r__ ake

__f__ ish

__v__ an

__j__ et

____ ipper

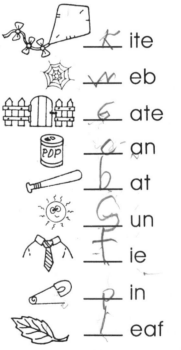

__k__ ite

__w__ eb

__g__ ate

__c__ an

__b__ at

__s__ un

__t__ ie

__p__ in

__l__ eaf

Challenge! Which letter begins 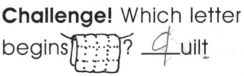? __q__ uilt

Circle the letter that makes the beginning sound. Then write the letter.

p (n)   (c) t   (h) j   z (v)

___   ___   ___   ___

p (l)   (b) d   g (r)   (k) y

___   ___   ___   ___

r (z)   (s) c   t (g)   (m) s

___   ___   ___   ___

(f) n   r (j)   n (w)   (q) n

___   ___   ___   ___

(d) k   n (t)   (y) w   g (p)

___   ___   ___   ___

Follow It to the End

Draw a line from each picture to the letter that makes the ending sound. Then write the missing letter.

b   k   d   g   m   f   s

roc_K_   cra_b_   bu_g_   toa_d_   gras_s_   wor_m_   lea_f_

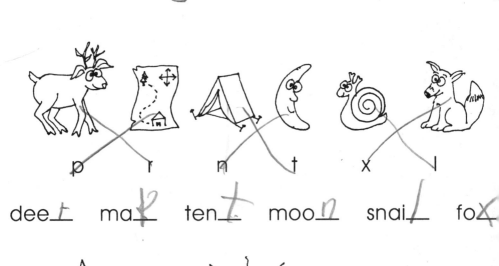

p   r   n   t   x   l

dee_r_   ma_p_   ten_t_   moo_n_   snai_l_   fo_x_

Which object wouldn't be found in the woods? ___crab___

ending sounds

Say the name of each picture. Then write the letter that makes the ending sound.

lo_g_

a_x_

co_t_

clou_d_

duc_k_

ca_p_

pa_n_

cu_b_

sta_r_

pai_l_

bu_s_

roo_f_

mushroo_m_

You made it!

Don't Clam Up

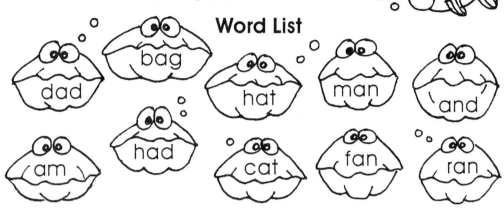

Word List

bag
dad
hat
man
and
am
had
cat
fan
ran

Write each word. Spell as you write.

1. _____   6. _____

2. _____   7. _____

3. _____   8. _____

4. _____   9. _____

5. _____   10. _____

Write the word that names each picture.

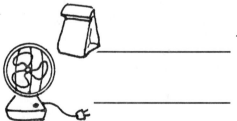

_____   _____

_____    _____

Use the Word List to write the words that rhyme.

man

_____   _____

dad   cat

_____   _____

Write the words that do not rhyme.

_____   _____

_____

Challenge! Use the letters **s**, **j**, and **t** to write a word that rhymes with each word.

am _____

bag _____

and _____

Cap Those Words

Word List

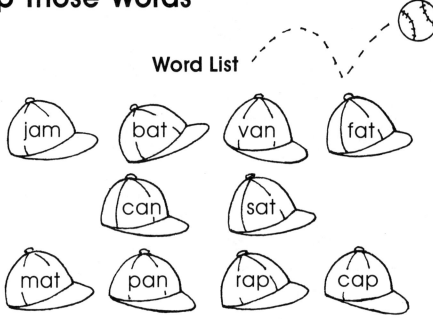

jam bat van fat can sat mat pan rap cap

Write the missing word in each sentence.

1. Please open the _____ of cat food.
2. He has a new blue and yellow _____ .
3. Hit the ball with the _____ .
4. That pig is very _____ .
5. Do you like _____ on your toast?
6. The cat sleeps on the _____ .
7. Put the _____ on the stove.
8. I heard a _____ at the door.
9. We rode in a _____ .
10. She _____ on the grass.

Unscramble the letters and write the word.

vna _____

tab _____

tsa _____

atm _____

maj _____

pac _____

apr _____

tfa _____

nac _____

nap _____

Unscramble the words and write the complete sentence.

| van. | the | He | in | sat |

_____

_____

Jetting Around

Word List

wet   best   beg   set

pet   jet   web   den   leg   nest

Read each clue. Then use the Word List to write the word.

1. To ask   _____

2. A spider spins it.   _____

3. You can fly in it.   _____

4. A bird lives in it.   _____

5. Not dry   _____

6. A part of your body   _____

7. To put down   _____

8. Better than everything   _____

9. An animal can be one.   _____

10. A room in a house   _____

Read the word on each tag. Use the Word List
to write the words that rhyme.

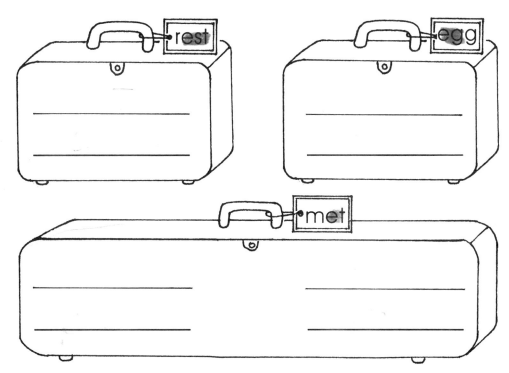

Write the two words that **do not** rhyme.

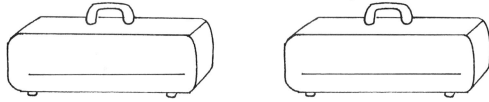

Write the sentence correctly by using a capital
letter at the beginning and a period at the end.

the   jet   will   on   ride   a   pet

_____

_____

Don't Be Penned In

Word List

get

bed

let

hen

fed

send

went

yes

pen

net

Write both groups of words in ABC order.
Hint: Look at the first letter of each word.

1. _____
2. _____
3. _____
4. _____
5. _____

1. _____
2. _____
3. _____
4. _____
5. _____

Use the Word List to write the missing word in each sentence. Then draw a line from the hen to her nest in the same order as your answers.

1. You sleep in a _____.

2. The _____ sat on her nest.

3. I will _____ a letter to my friend.

4. Ed _____ the dog.

5. Lift the shade to _____ in the sun.

6. You can write with a _____.

7. Please _____ me a glass of milk.

8. We _____ to the zoo.

9. Meg caught a butterfly in her _____.

10. Mom said, ''_____, you may go play!''

bed	hen	set	went	net
	send	let	get	yes
web	fed	best	pen	

Limbering Up

Write the letter of the correct word beside its matching picture. Then write the word.

Word List

a. fin   _h_   _____sit_____

b. hit   ____   _____

c. lid   ____   _____

d. pig   ____   _____

e. mix   ____   _____

f. pin   ____   _____

g. wig   ____   _____

h. sit   ____   _____

i. win   ____   _____

j. dig   ____   _____

Use the Word List to write each word where it belongs.

Name Words

Action Words

_____

_____

_____

_____

_____

_____

_____

_____

_____

_____

Write the sentence correctly. Use a capital letter at the beginning and a question mark at the end.

pig   the   will   win

_____

Pitch a Few Words

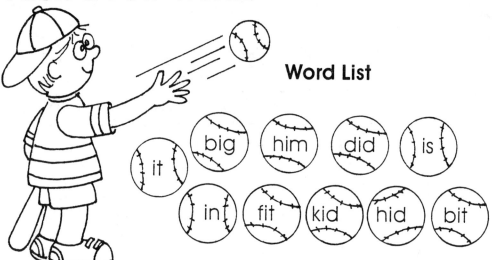

Word List

Write the words that rhyme with each picture.

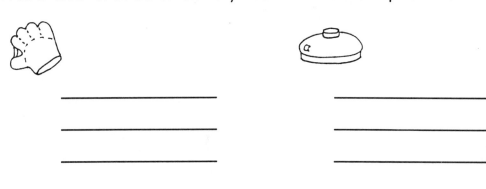

Which two words **do not** rhyme with any of the pictures?

Unscramble the words to write a complete sentence.

1. it   Did   him?   fit

_____

2. it.   bit   The   pig

_____

3. the   fit?   Did   wig

_____

4. kid.   He   big   is   a

_____

5. it   the   He   in   hid   cap.

_____

Use the Word List to write the words that begin with the same sound as the pictures.

_____   _____

_____   _____

_____   _____   _____

Shopping Spree

Word List

mop	box	rod
pop	top	sock
cot	doll	pot
	lock	

Match each picture with a word from the Word List.

_____   _____   _____

_____   _____   _____

_____   _____   _____

Which object would you buy? _____

Read each clue. Use the Word List to complete the shopping list puzzle.

Across
2. toy that looks like a person
4. knitted covering for the foot
6. container used for cooking
7. cone-shaped toy that spins

Down
1. used to catch fish
3. a key will open one
5. a narrow canvas fold-up bed
6. a soft drink

Which two words are not in the puzzle?

_____   _____

Write as many new words as you can that rhyme with the words on the coupon. Count one point for each word. Write the number in the box.

BONUS COUPON	cot	pop	rod	
	_____	_____	_____	Bonus Points
	_____	_____	_____	
	_____	_____	_____	☐
	_____	_____	_____	

Hot off the Press

Word List

got	mom	hop
hot	rock	on	not
lot	stop	dot

Oops! Use the Word List to find and circle each hidden word. Then write it on the line.

1. spgotwn _____

2. dotxzn _____

3. fahotrd _____

4. quimomz _____

5. clostop _____

6. dronder _____

7. shuzhopp _____

8. lonotrx _____

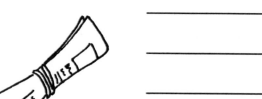

9. escrock _____

10. rulotmer _____

You are the editor. Circle the words that are misspelled. Then write them correctly.

One hut day Mom saw a white det on the grass. It was Poppy the rabbit. He liked to hup in the grass. He was having a lat of fun. Mon tried to catch him, but he would nat stup. At last he jumped en tup of a box. Mom gat him and put him in his pen.

Write the sentence correctly.

will   the   rabbit   hop   to   mom

_____

_____

Did you begin the sentence with a capital letter?
Did you put a question mark at the end?
Did you capitalize "Mom"?

Take a Bus Ride

Word List

sun	but	bus	run	fun	cut
us	up	nut	duck		

Use the Word List to write the missing word on the line.

1. Our teacher said we must walk, not _____.

2. We got on the _____.

3. The _____ was shining and it was hot.

4. Bud fell down and _____ his hand.

5. We helped him get _____.

6. He thanked _____.

7. We saw a chipmunk eating a _____.

8. There was a _____ on the pond.

9. Justin found a bug, _____ he let it go.

10. We had lots of _____ on the bus trip.

Help Rusty find his way back to the bus. Read each clue and write the correct word on the line. Then trace a path from Rusty to the bus in the same order as your answers.

You ride in it.

_____

An animal

_____

A good time

_____

bus   duck

You and me

_____

hug   cup   fun

Not down

_____

up   us   luck

Move very fast.

_____

jug   run   but

Not this, ____ that

_____

mud   nut

You can eat it.

_____

sun

It is in the sky.

_____

rug

These ✂ will do this.

_____

cut   drum

Puppy Pranks

cup · drum · dug · jug · mud · mug · tub · bug · rug · tug

Match each picture with a sentence and write the missing word.

1. Dusty the pup licks a _____.

2. There is a _____ on the pup.

3. Lucky the pup is sitting on top of a

   _____.

4. Rusty the pup will _____ on a rope.

5. Buddy the pup jumped inside a _____

6. Plump the pup walks in the _____.

7. Buck the pup splashes in the _____.

8. Tucker the pup _____ a hole.

9. Cuddles the pup is under a _____.

10. Gus the pup tipped over the _____.

Use the Word List to unscramble the letters on the blocks. Write the word on the line.

One puppy on page 24 did not have a name. Give the puppy a name with a /**ŭ**/ sound.

_____

Review

Pages 2-9 Write the /ă/ word that names each picture. Circle the beginning sound. Draw a line under the ending sound.

_____   _____

_____   _____

_____   _____

_____   _____

_____   _____

Pages 10-13 Use /ĕ/ with the other letters to spell the missing words.

e   n   f   s   h   w   j   d   g   b   t

1. He _____ corn to the pigs.

2. It is time to go to _____.

3. You can catch a butterfly with a

   _____.

4. Please _____ some jam at the store.

5. There are two eggs in the _____.

6. The _____ sat on the eggs.

7. The puppy got _____ in the rain.

8. Do you like to fly in a _____?

Pages 14-17 Read each clue. Use the letters to help you write the correct /ĭ/ word.

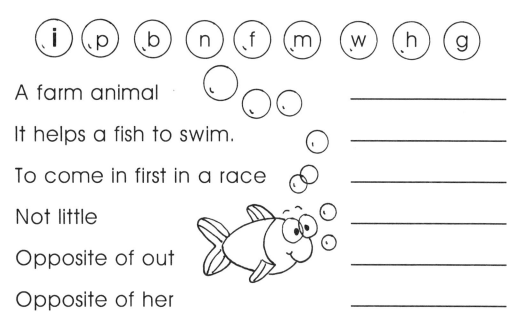

(i) (p) (b) (n) (f) (m) (w) (h) (g)

A farm animal _____

It helps a fish to swim. _____

To come in first in a race _____

Not little _____

Opposite of out _____

Opposite of her _____

Pages 18-25 Circle all the /ŏ/ and /ŭ/ words. Write each word under the correct heading.

d	c	u	p	b	u	s	g	o	t
r	m	o	p	s	o	c	k	z	u
u	u	s	o	f	u	n	o	p	p
m	o	n	l	o	c	k	m	o	m

/ŏ/   /ŭ/

_____ _____   _____ _____

_____ _____   _____ _____

_____ _____   _____ _____

Put on the Brakes!

Word List

made		bake
name	game	gave
ate	take	came
same	gate	

Read each clue. Write the correct word(s) from the Word List.

1. It begins like 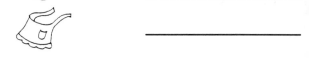 _____

2. It begins like _____

3. It begins like _____

4. It begins like 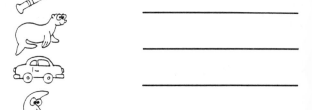 _____

5. It begins like _____

6. It begins like  _____

7. It begins like  _____

8. It begins like _____

_____

_____

Whew!
What letter does
each word
end with? _____

Use the Word List to circle each word in the
puzzle.
Look →.

t	a	k	e	b	s	a	m	e	n
p	g	a	t	e	e	b	a	k	e
g	a	m	e	d	g	a	v	e	f
n	m	a	d	e	j	c	a	m	e
k	n	q	a	t	e	m	p	r	l

Write the words you circled.

_____   _____

_____   _____

_____   _____

_____   _____

_____

Which word isn't in the puzzle? _____

Write your first and last name.

_____

A Relay Race

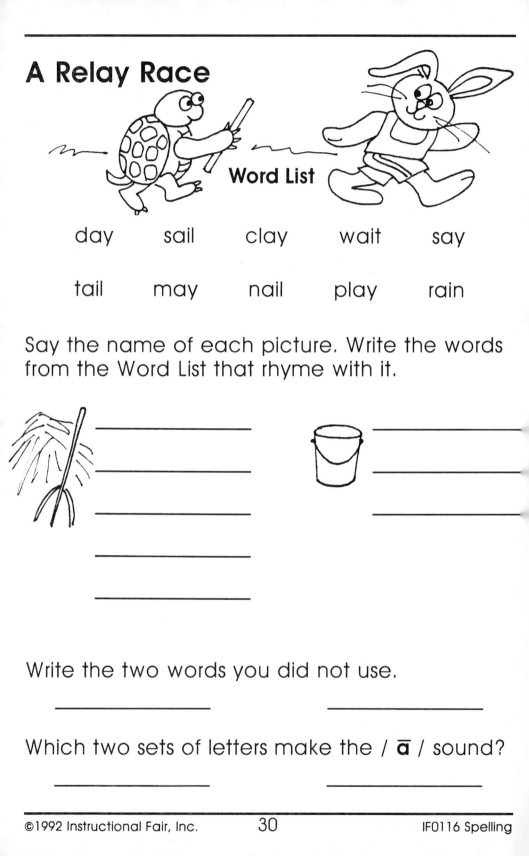

Word List

day	sail	clay	wait	say
tail	may	nail	play	rain

Say the name of each picture. Write the words from the Word List that rhyme with it.

_____

_____

_____

_____

_____

_____

_____

_____

Write the two words you did not use.

_____   _____

Which two sets of letters make the / ā / sound?

_____   _____

Use the Word List to write the missing word in each sentence. Write one letter on each line.

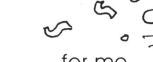

1. Please __ __ __ __ for me.
   ‾1

2. A happy dog wags its __ __ __ __.
   ‾‾‾2

3. Hit the __ __ __ __ with a hammer.
   ‾‾‾3

4. Do you like to __ __ __ __ in the sand?
   ‾‾‾4

5. We like to __ __ __ __ on the lake.
   ‾‾‾5

6. What did he __ __ __?
   ‾‾‾6

7. __ __ __ we go to the park now?
   ‾7

8. Can you make a snail out of __ __ __ __?
   ‾‾‾8

9. Jane got wet playing in the __ __ __ __.
   ‾‾‾9

10. What __ __ __ is it?
    ‾10

Use the numbered letters to solve the code.

__ __ __ __ __ ! __ O U
6 3 4 4 8   7

__ __ __ __ __ __ __ __ !
10 5 10   1 3 9   5 2

Sweeping Along

Write the words in which the / ē / sound is made with only one e.

_____   _____

_____   _____

Write the words in which the / ē / sound is made with two e's together.

_____   _____

_____   _____

_____   _____

Which words name people?

_____ _____ _____ _____

Which word names an insect? _____

Which two words are about plants?

_____   _____

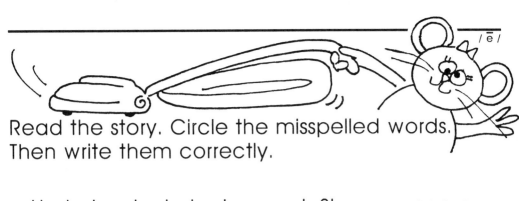

Read the story. Circle the misspelled words. Then write them correctly.

Ha helped mi plant a sood. Sha can cee a bea buzzing in the garden. Wo meed to pull up the wede. We feal good about our garden.

_____ _____

_____ _____

_____

_____ _____

_____

"Clean up" this sentence. Unscramble the words and write the complete sentence.

| you | How | feel | do | today? |

_____

_____

Write a complete sentence to tell what you would plant in a garden.

_____

_____

Sealing Seals

Word List

1st Prize

eat   leaf   leap

meat   neat   read

seal   seat   lead   sea

Read each clue. Write the correct word(s).

Begins like [ear]

Begins like [eel]

Begins like [rain]

_____

_____

_____

Begins like [ladder]

Begins like [nail]

Begins like [sock]

_____

Good Work!

_____

_____

_____

Which two letters are the same in every word?

_____

Use the Word List to write the words where they belong.

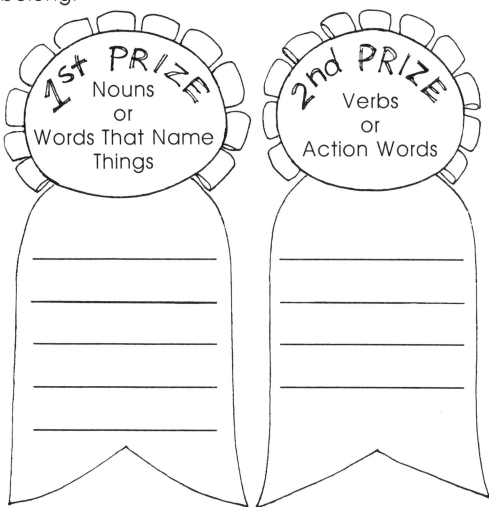

1st PRIZE
Nouns
or
Words That Name
Things

2nd PRIZE
Verbs
or
Action Words

Which word does not belong? _____

Write a sentence using the word that does not belong.

_____

_____

Filing System

Word List

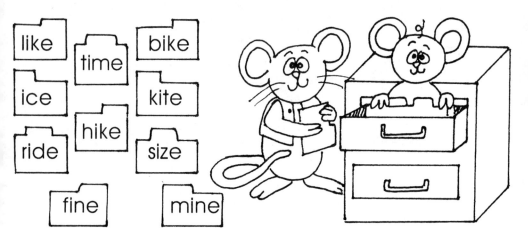

like
time
bike
ice
kite
ride
hike
size
fine
mine

Use the Word List to unscramble the letters and write each word.

m i t e _____

n e m i _____

e l k i _____

d r i e _____

e c i _____

n i f e _____

k e b i _____

e k i h _____

i z s e _____

t k i e _____

Answer Key

Spelling
Homework Booklet
Grade 1

Start the Race!

Letter Bank

Say the name of each picture. Then write the letter that makes the beginning sound.

h and   k ite
y arn   w eb
n est   g ate
m at   c an
d og   b at
r ake   s un
f ish   t ie
v an   p in
j et   l eaf
z ipper

Challenge! Which letter begins q uilt

©1992 Instructional Fair, Inc.   2   IF0116 Spelling

Circle the letter that makes the beginning sound. Then write the letter.

©1992 Instructional Fair, Inc.   3   IF0116 Spelling

Follow It to the End

Draw a line from each picture to the letter that makes the ending sound. Then write the missing letter.

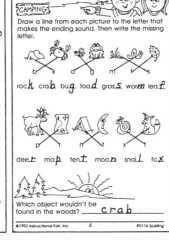

rock   crab   bug   toad   grass   worm   leaf

deer   map   tent   moon   snail   fox

Which object wouldn't be found in the woods? __crab__

©1992 Instructional Fair, Inc.   4   IF0116 Spelling

Say the name of each picture. Then write the letter that makes the ending sound.

lo g   a x   co t
clou d   duc k   ca p
pa n   cu b   sta r
pai l   bu s   roo f
mushroo m   You made it!

©1992 Instructional Fair, Inc.   5   IF0116 Spelling

Don't Clam Up

Word List: bag, dad, hat, man, and, had, am, cat, fan, ran

Write each word. Spell as you write.

1. dad
2. bag
3. hat
4. man
5. and
6. am
7. had
8. cat
9. fan
10. ran

Write the word that names each picture.

bag   cat
fan   hat

©1992 Instructional Fair, Inc.   6   IF0116 Spelling

Use the Word List to write the words that rhyme.

man

ran   fan

dad   cat

had   hat

Write the words that do not rhyme.

am   and

bag

Challenge! Use the letters s, j, and t to write a word that rhymes with each word.

am   jam
bag   tag
and   sand

©1992 Instructional Fair, Inc.   7   IF0116 Spelling

Cap Those Words

Word List: jam, bat, van, fat, can, sat, mat, pan, rap, cap

Write the missing word in each sentence.

1. Please open the __can__ of cat food.
2. He has a new blue and yellow __cap__.
3. Hit the ball with the __bat__.
4. That pig is very __fat__.
5. Do you like __jam__ on your toast?
6. The cat sleeps on the __mat__.
7. Put the __pan__ on the stove.
8. I heard a __rap__ at the door.
9. We rode in a __van__.
10. She __sat__ on the grass.

©1992 Instructional Fair, Inc.   8   IF0116 Spelling

Unscramble the letters and write the word.

vna	_van_	tab	_bat_
tsa	_sat_	atm	_mat_
maj	_jam_	pac	_cap_
apr	_rap_	tfa	_fat_
nac	_can_	nap	_pan_

Unscramble the words and write the complete sentence.

van. the He in sat

He sat in the van.

Jetting Around

Word List

wet best beg set
pet jet web den leg nest

Read each clue. Then use the Word List to write the word.

1. To ask — _beg_
2. A spider spins it. — _web_
3. You can fly in it. — _jet_
4. A bird lives in it. — _nest_
5. Not dry — _wet_
6. A part of your body — _leg_
7. To put down — _set_
8. Better than everything — _best_
9. An animal can be one. — _pet_
10. A room in a house — _den_

Read the word on each tag. Use the Word List to write the words that rhyme.

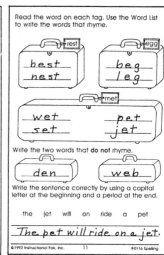

rest — _best_ / _nest_
egg — _beg_ / _leg_
met — _wet_ / _set_ — _pet_ / _jet_

Write the two words that **do not** rhyme.

den   _web_

Write the sentence correctly by using a capital letter at the beginning and a period at the end.

the jet will on ride a pet

The pet will ride on a jet.

Don't Be Penned In

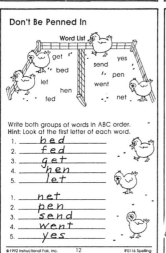

Word List

get   yes
bed   send
let   pen
hen   went
fed   net

Write both groups of words in ABC order.
Hint: Look at the first letter of each word.

1. _bed_
2. _fed_
3. _get_
4. _hen_
5. _let_

1. _net_
2. _pen_
3. _send_
4. _went_
5. _yes_

Use the Word List to write the missing word in each sentence. Then draw a line from the hen to her nest in the same order as your answers.

1. You sleep in a _bed_.
2. The _hen_ sat on her nest.
3. I will _send_ a letter to my friend.
4. Ed _fed_ the dog.
5. Lift the shade to _let_ in the sun.
6. You can write with a _pen_.
7. Please _get_ me a glass of milk.
8. We _went_ to the zoo.
9. Meg caught a butterfly in her _net_.
10. Mom said, "_Yes_, you may go play!"

bed hen set went net

send let get yes

web fed best pen

Limbering Up

Write the letter of each word beside the matching picture. Then write the word.

Word List

a. fin
b. hit
c. lid
d. pig
e. mix
f. pin
g. wig
h. sit
i. win
j. dig

_h_ — _sit_
_c_ — _lid_
_g_ — _wig_
_f_ — _pin_
_b_ — _hit_
_d_ — _pig_
_e_ — _mix_
_a_ — _fin_
_j_ — _dig_
_i_ — _win_

Use the Word List to write each word where it belongs.

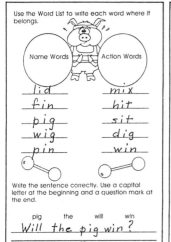

Name Words   Action Words

lid   _mix_
fin   _hit_
pig   _sit_
wig   _dig_
pin   _win_

Write the sentence correctly. Use a capital letter at the beginning and a question mark at the end.

pig the will win

Will the pig win?

Pitch a Few Words

Word List

it big him did is
in fit kid hid bit

Write the words that rhyme with each picture.

_it_   _did_
bit   _hid_
fit   _kid_

big   _in_

Which two words do **not** rhyme with any of the pictures?

_is_   _him_

Unscramble the words to write a complete sentence.

1. it Did him? fit
Did it fit him?
2. it. bit The pig
The pig bit it.
3. the fit? Did wig
Did the wig fit?
4. kid. He big is a
He is a big kid.
5. it the He in hid cap.
He hid it in the cap.
or—_He hid the cap in it._

Use the Word List to write the words that begin with the same sound as the pictures.

him   _hid_
big   _bit_
_in_   _is_   _it_

IF0116 Answer Key

Shopping Spree

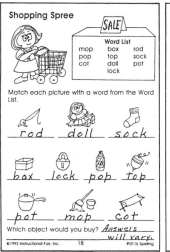

Word List
mop   box   rod
pop   top   sock
cot   doll   lock

Match each picture with a word from the Word List.

rod   _doll_   _sock_

box   _lock_   _pop_   _top_

pot   _mop_   _cot_

Which object would you buy? _Answers will vary._

Read each clue. Use the Word List to complete the shopping list puzzle.

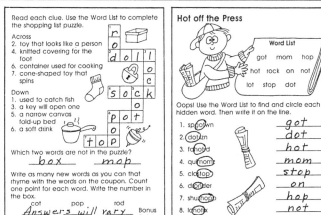

Across
2. toy that looks like a person
4. knitted covering for the foot
6. container used for cooking
7. cone-shaped toy that spins

Down
1. used to catch fish
3. a key will open one
5. a narrow canvas fold-up bed
6. a soft drink

Which two words are not in the puzzle?
box   _mop_

Write as many new words as you can that rhyme with the words on the coupon. Count one point for each word. Write the number in the box.

cot   pop   rod
Answers will vary   Bonus Points

Hot off the Press

Word List
got   mom   hop
hot   rock   on   not
lot   stop   dot

Oops! Use the Word List to find and circle each hidden word. Then write it on the line.

1. spgotwn   _got_
2. dotzn   _dot_
3. fohotd   _hot_
4. qumomr   _mom_
5. clostop   _stop_
6. dronder   _on_
7. shuhopb   _hop_
8. lahotx   _not_
9. esdrock   _rock_
10. rulotmer   _lot_

You are the editor. Circle the words that are misspelled. Then write them correctly.

One hut day Mom saw a white det on the grass. It was Poppy the rabbit. He liked to hup in the grass. He was having a lat of fun. Mom tried to catch him, but he would hat tup. At last he jumped en dup of a box. Mom gat him and put him in his pen.

hot   _not_
dot   _stop_
hop   _on_
lot   _top_
mom   _got_

Write the sentence correctly.
will   the   rabbit   hop   to   mom
Will the rabbit hop to Mom?

Did you begin the sentence with a capital letter?
Did you put a question mark at the end?
Did you capitalize "Mom"?

Take a Bus Ride

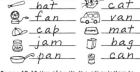

Word List
sun   but   bus   run   fun   cut
us   up   nut   duck

Use the Word List to write the missing word on the line.
1. Our teacher said we must walk, not _run_.
2. We got on the _bus_.
3. The _sun_ was shining and it was hot.
4. Bud fell down and _cut_ his hand.
5. We helped him get _up_.
6. He thanked _us_.
7. We saw a chipmunk eating a _nut_.
8. There was a _duck_ on the pond.
9. Justin found a bug, _but_ he let it go.
10. We had lots of _fun_ on the bus trip.

Help Rusty find his way back to the bus. Read each clue and write the correct word on the line. Then trace a path from Rusty to the bus in the same order as your answers.

You ride in it.   _bus_
An animal   _duck_
A good time   _fun_
You and me   _us_
Not down   _up_
Move very fast.   _run_
Not this, ___ that   _but_
You can eat it.   _nut_
It is in the sky.   _sun_
These ___ will do this.   _cut_

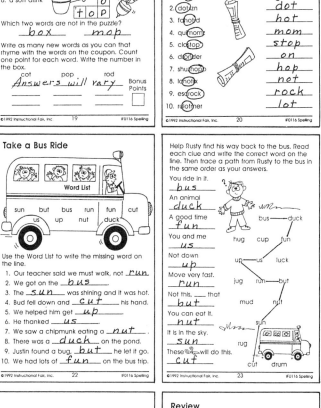

Puppy Pranks   Word List

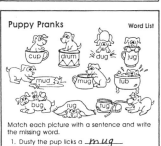

cup   drum   dug   jug
mud   mug   tub
bug   rug   tug

Match each picture with a sentence and write the missing word.
1. Dusty the pup licks a _mug_.
2. There is a _bug_ on the pup.
3. Lucky the pup is sitting on top of a _drum_.
4. Rusty the pup will _tug_ on a rope.
5. Buddy the pup looks inside a _jug_.
6. Plump the pup walks in the _mud_.
7. Buck the pup splashes in the _tub_.
8. Tucker the pup _dug_ a hole.
9. Cuddles the pup is under a _rug_.
10. Gus the pup tipped over the _cup_.

Use the Word List to unscramble the letters on the blocks. Write the word on the line.

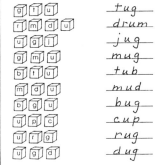

tug
drum
jug
mug
tub
mud
bug
cup
rug
dug

One puppy on page 24 did not have a name. Give the puppy a name with a /u̇/ sound.
Answers will vary

Review

Pages 2-9 Write the /ă/ word that names each picture. Circle the beginning sound. Draw a line under the ending sound.

hat   _cat_
fan   _van_
cap   _mat_
jam   _bag_
pan   _can_

Pages 10-13 Use /ĕ/ with the other letters to spell the missing words.
e n f s h w j d g b t
1. He _fed_ corn to the pigs.
2. It is time to go to _bed_.
3. You can catch a butterfly with a _net_.
4. Please _get_ some jam at the store.
5. There are two eggs in the _nest_.
6. The _hen_ sat on the eggs.
7. The puppy got _wet_ in the rain.
8. Do you like to fly in a _jet_?

IF0116 Answer Key

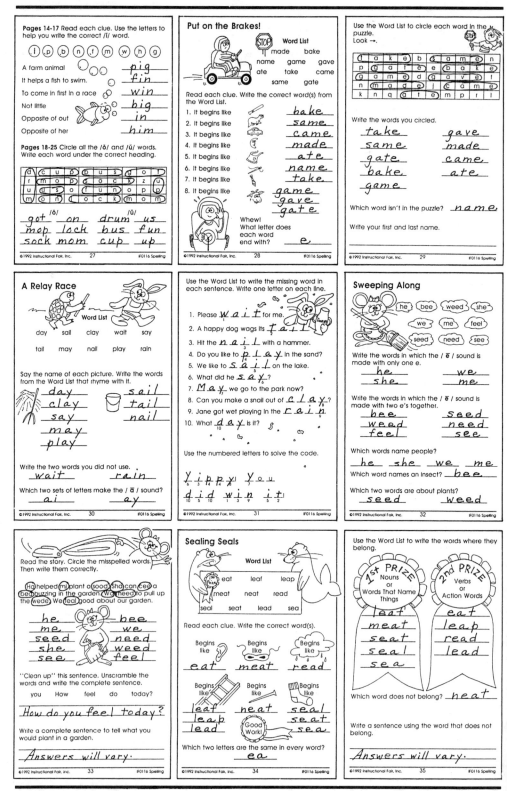

Pages 14-17 Read each clue. Use the letters to help you write the correct /ĭ/ word.

(i) (p) (b) (n) (f) (m) (w) (h) (g)

A farm animal	pig
It helps a fish to swim.	fin
To come in first in a race	win
Not little	big
Opposite of out	in
Opposite of her	him

Pages 18-25 Circle all the /ŏ/ and /ŭ/ words. Write each word under the correct heading.

/ŏ/		/ŭ/	
got	on	drum	us
mop	lock	bus	fun
sock	mom	cup	up

©1992 Instructional Fair, Inc.   27   IF0116 Spelling

Put on the Brakes!

Word List
made   bake
name   game   gave
ate   take   came
same   gate

Read each clue. Write the correct word(s) from the Word List.

1. It begins like   bake
2. It begins like   same
3. It begins like   came
4. It begins like   made
5. It begins like   ate
6. It begins like   name
7. It begins like   take
8. It begins like   game gave gate

Whew! What letter does each word end with?   e

©1992 Instructional Fair, Inc.   28   IF0116 Spelling

Use the Word List to circle each word in the puzzle. Look →.

Write the words you circled.

take	gave
same	made
gate	came
bake	ate
game	

Which word isn't in the puzzle?   name

Write your first and last name.

©1992 Instructional Fair, Inc.   29   IF0116 Spelling

A Relay Race

Word List
day   sail   clay   wait   say
tail   may   nail   play   rain

Say the name of each picture. Write the words from the Word List that rhyme with it.

day	sail
clay	tail
say	nail
may	
play	

Write the two words you did not use.
wait   rain

Which two sets of letters make the /ā/ sound?
ai   ay

©1992 Instructional Fair, Inc.   30   IF0116 Spelling

Use the Word List to write the missing word in each sentence. Write one letter on each line.

1. Please w a i t for me.
2. A happy dog wags its t a i l.
3. Hit the n a i l with a hammer.
4. Do you like to p l a y in the sand?
5. We like to s a i l on the lake.
6. What did he s a y?
7. M a y we go to the park now?
8. Can you make a snail out of c l a y?
9. Jane got wet playing in the r a i n.
10. What d a y is it?

Use the numbered letters to solve the code.

Y i p p y   Y o u
d i d   w i n   i t

©1992 Instructional Fair, Inc.   31   IF0116 Spelling

Sweeping Along

he bee weed she
we me feel
seed need see

Write the words in which the /ē/ sound is made with only one e.
he   we
she   me

Write the words in which the /ē/ sound is made with two e's together.
bee   seed
weed   need
feel   see

Which words name people?
he   she   we   me

Which word names an insect?   bee

Which two words are about plants?
seed   weed

©1992 Instructional Fair, Inc.   32   IF0116 Spelling

Read the story. Circle the misspelled words. Then write them correctly.

He helped me plant a good. She can see a bee buzzing in the garden. We need to pull up the weed. We feel good about our garden.

he	bee
me	we
seed	need
she	weed
see	feel

"Clean up" this sentence. Unscramble the words and write the complete sentence.

you   How   feel   do   today?

How do you feel today?

Write a complete sentence to tell what you would plant in a garden.

Answers will vary.

©1992 Instructional Fair, Inc.   33   IF0116 Spelling

Sealing Seals

Word List
eat   leaf   leap
meat   neat   read
seal   seat   lead   sea

Read each clue. Write the correct word(s).

Begins like   eat
Begins like   meat
Begins like   read

Begins like   leaf   seal
leap   seat
lead   sea

Which two letters are the same in every word?   ea

©1992 Instructional Fair, Inc.   34   IF0116 Spelling

Use the Word List to write the words where they belong.

1st PRIZE — Nouns or Words That Name Things
leaf
meat
seat
seal
sea

2nd PRIZE — Verbs or Action Words
eat
leap
read
lead

Which word does not belong?   neat

Write a sentence using the word that does not belong.

Answers will vary.

©1992 Instructional Fair, Inc.   35   IF0116 Spelling

©1992 Instructional Fair, Inc.   IF0116 Answer Key

Filing System

Word List

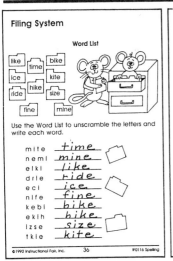

like, time, bike, ice, kite, ride, hike, size, fine, mine

Use the Word List to unscramble the letters and write each word.

m i t e _time_
n e m l _mine_
e l k l _like_
d r l e _ride_
e c l _ice_
n l f e _fine_
k e b l _bike_
e k l h _hike_
l z s e _size_
t k l e _kite_

Write the words from page 36 in ABC order.

bike
fine
hike
ice
kite
like
mine
ride
size
time

Write a complete sentence telling about something that you like to do.

Answers will vary.

Eyeing the Sky

Word List

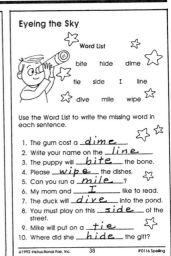

bite, hide, dime, tie, side, I, line, dive, mile, wipe

Use the Word List to write the missing word in each sentence.

1. The gum cost a _dime_
2. Write your name on the _line_
3. The puppy will _bite_ the bone.
4. Please _wipe_ the dishes.
5. Can you run a _mile_ ?
6. My mom and _I_ like to read.
7. The duck will _dive_ into the pond.
8. You must play on this _side_ of the street.
9. Mike will put on a _tie_
10. Where did she _hide_ the gift?

Use the Word List to circle the hidden words. Then write each word on the line.

1. crum(bite) _bite_
2. d(I)erald _I_
3. sr(hide)sh _hide_
4. ts(side)els _side_
5. b(tie)nd _tie_
6. ga(line)ds _line_
7. sk(wipe)r _wipe_
8. w(mile)s _mile_
9. s(dime)nap _dime_
10. me(dive)r _dive_

Choose two words from the Word List and write them in a sentence.

Answers will vary.

Motoring Home

Word List

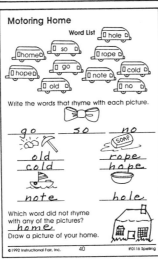

hole, so, rope, home, go, cold, hope, note, no, old

Write the words that rhyme with each picture.

_go_ _so_ _no_
old _rope_
cold _hope_
note _hole_

Which word did not rhyme with any of the pictures?
home
Draw a picture of your home.

Read the clues. Use the Word List to complete the puzzle.

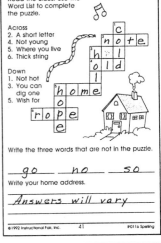

Across
2. A short letter
4. Not young
5. Where you live
6. Thick string

Down
1. Not hot
3. You can dig one
5. Wish for

Crossword answers: note, old, cold, home, rope

Write the three words that are not in the puzzle.

_go_ _no_ _so_

Write your home address.

Answers will vary

Go for the Goal

Word List

boat, goat, loaf, road, soap, toad, toast, coat, oats, load

Read the clues. Write the correct word(s).

1. It begins like _load_ _loaf_
2. It begins like _oats_
3. It begins like _coat_
4. It begins like _soap_
5. It begins like _boat_
6. It begins like _goat_
7. It begins like _road_
8. It begins like _toad_ _toast_

What two letters are the same in every word?
_oa_

Use the Word List to complete the puzzle.

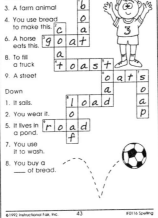

Across
3. A farm animal
4. You use bread to make this.
6. A horse eats this.
8. To fill a truck
9. A street

Down
1. It sails.
2. You wear it.
5. It lives in a pond.
7. You use it to wash.
8. You buy a ____ of bread.

Crossword answers: goat, toast, oats, load, oats, boat, coat, road, soap, loaf

---

Review

Pages 28-31 Write the / ā / word that names each picture.

1. _nail_
2. _game_
3. _play_
4. _bake_
5. _gate_
6. _rain_
7. _tail_
8. _sail_

Pages 32-35 Use the code to write the missing / ē / word in each sentence.

e	a	s	l	b	f	n	t	d	m
1	2	3	4	5	6	7	8	9	10

1. A _seal_ lives in the sea.
2. The _bee_ buzzed around the flower.
3. How do you _feel_ ?
4. He keeps his room very _neat_
5. We planted a _seed_
6. Do you like to eat _meat_ ?
7. Will you come to the park with _me_ ?
8. The _leaf_ fell off the tree.

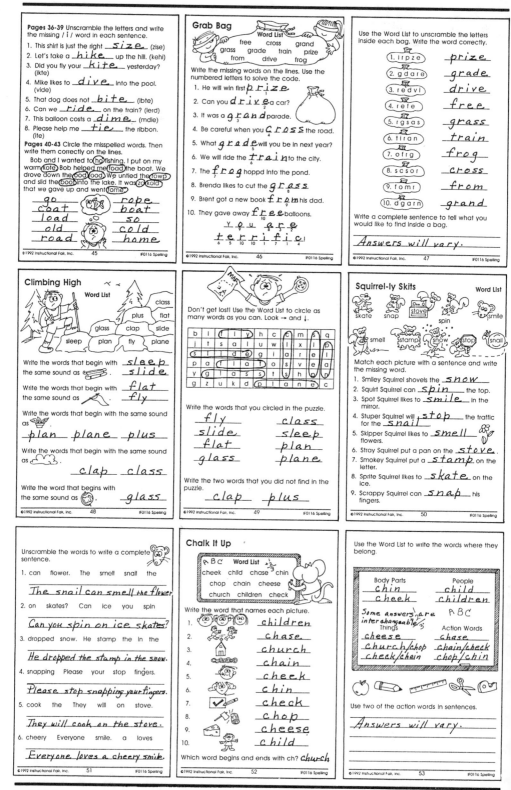

Pages 36-39 (panel, p.45)

Pages 36-39 Unscramble the letters and write the missing / ĭ / word in each sentence.

1. This shirt is just the right _size_ (zise)
2. Let's take a _hike_ up the hill. (kehi)
3. Did you fly your _kite_ yesterday? (ikte)
4. Mike likes to _dive_ into the pool. (vide)
5. That dog does not _bite_. (ibte)
6. Can we _ride_ on the train? (lerd)
7. This balloon costs a _dime_. (mdie)
8. Please help me _tie_ the ribbon. (ite)

Pages 40-43 Circle the misspelled words. Then write them correctly on the lines.

Bob and I wanted to go fishing. I put on my warm kote. Bob helped me loadd the boat. We drove down the rood. We untied the towp and slid the boob into the lake. It was zo kold that we gave up and went hoome.

go — rope
coat — boat
load — so
old — cold
road — home

©1992 Instructional Fair, Inc. 45 IF0116 Spelling

Grab Bag (p.46)

Word List
free cross grand
grass grade train prize
from drive frog

Write the missing words on the lines. Use the numbered letters to solve the code.

1. He will win first _prize_
2. Can you _drive_ a car?
3. It was a _grand_ parade.
4. Be careful when you _cross_ the road.
5. What _grade_ will you be in next year?
6. We will ride the _train_ to the city.
7. The _frog_ hoppd into the pond.
8. Brenda likes to cut the _grass_.
9. Brent got a new book _from_ his dad.
10. They gave away _free_ balloons.

You are terrific!

©1992 Instructional Fair, Inc. 46 IF0116 Spelling

(p.47)

Use the Word List to unscramble the letters inside each bag. Write the word correctly.

1. irpze — _prize_
2. gdare — _grade_
3. redvi — _drive_
4. refe — _free_
5. rgsas — _grass_
6. tiran — _train_
7. ofrg — _frog_
8. scsor — _cross_
9. fomr — _from_
10. dgarn — _grand_

Write a complete sentence to tell what you would like to find inside a bag.

Answers will vary.

©1992 Instructional Fair, Inc. 47 IF0116 Spelling

Climbing High (p.48)

Word List
class
plus flat
glass clap slide
sleep plan fly plane

Write the words that begin with the same sound as. _sleep_ _slide_

Write the words that begin with the same sound as. _flat_ _fly_

Write the words that begin with the same sound as. _plan_ _plane_ _plus_

Write the words that begin with the same sound as. _clap_ _class_

Write the word that begins with the same sound as. _glass_

©1992 Instructional Fair, Inc. 48 IF0116 Spelling

(p.49)

Don't get lost! Use the Word List to circle as many words as you can. Look → and ↓.

Write the words that you circled in the puzzle.

fly _class_
slide _sleep_
flat _plan_
glass _plane_

Write the two words that you did not find in the puzzle.

clap _plus_

©1992 Instructional Fair, Inc. 49 IF0116 Spelling

Squirrel-ly Skits (p.50)

Word List
skate snap stove spin smile snail
smell stamp snow stop

Match each picture with a sentence and write the missing word.

1. Smiley Squirrel shovels the _snow_
2. Squirt Squirrel can _spin_ the top.
3. Spot Squirrel likes to _smile_ in the mirror.
4. Stuper Squirrel will _stop_ the traffic for the _snail_
5. Skipper Squirrel likes to _smell_ flowers.
6. Stray Squirrel put a pan on the _stove_.
7. Smokey Squirrel put a _stamp_ on the letter.
8. Sprite Squirrel likes to _skate_ on the ice.
9. Scrappy Squirrel can _snap_ his fingers.

©1992 Instructional Fair, Inc. 50 IF0116 Spelling

(p.51)

Unscramble the words to write a complete sentence.

1. can flower. The smell snail the
The snail can smell the flower.

2. on skates? Can ice you spin
Can you spin on ice skates?

3. dropped snow. He stamp the in the
He dropped the stamp in the snow.

4. snapping Please your stop fingers.
Please stop snapping your fingers.

5. cook the They will on stove.
They will cook on the stove.

6. cheery Everyone smile. a loves
Everyone loves a cheery smile.

©1992 Instructional Fair, Inc. 51 IF0116 Spelling

Chalk It Up (p.52)

Word List
cheek child chase chin
chop chain cheese
church children check

Write the word that names each picture.

1. _children_
2. _chase_
3. _church_
4. _chain_
5. _cheek_
6. _chin_
7. _check_
8. _chop_
9. _cheese_
10. _child_

Which word begins and ends with ch? _church_

©1992 Instructional Fair, Inc. 52 IF0116 Spelling

(p.53)

Use the Word List to write the words where they belong.

Body Parts	People
chin	child
cheek	children

Some answers are interchangeable.

Things	Action Words
cheese	chase
church/chop	chain/check
check/chain	chop/chin

Use two of the action words in sentences.

Answers will vary.

©1992 Instructional Fair, Inc. 53 IF0116 Spelling

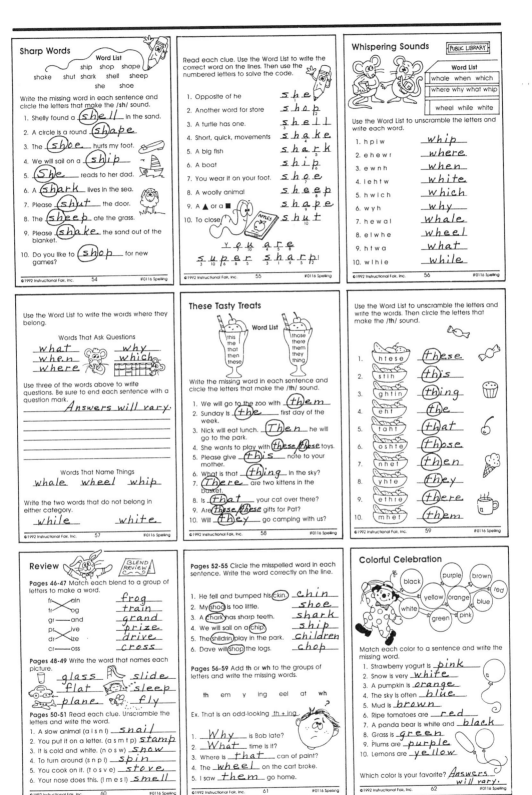

Sharp Words

Word List
ship shop shape
shake shut shark shell sheep
she shoe

Write the missing word in each sentence and circle the letters that make the /sh/ sound.

1. Shelly found a (sh)ell in the sand.
2. A circle is a round (sh)ape.
3. The (sh)oe hurts my foot.
4. We will sail on a (sh)ip.
5. (Sh)e reads to her dad.
6. A (sh)ark lives in the sea.
7. Please (sh)ut the door.
8. The (sh)eep ate the grass.
9. Please (sh)ake the sand out of the blanket.
10. Do you like to (sh)op for new games?

©1992 Instructional Fair, Inc.   54   IF0116 Spelling

Read each clue. Use the Word List to write the correct word on the lines. Then use the numbered letters to solve the code.

1. Opposite of he — s h e
2. Another word for store — s h o p
3. A turtle has one. — s h e l l
4. Short, quick, movements — s h a k e
5. A big fish — s h a r k
6. A boat — s h i p
7. You wear it on your foot. — s h o e
8. A woolly animal — s h e e p
9. A ▲ or a ■ — s h a p e
10. To close — s h u t

y o u   a r e
s u p e r   s h a r p !

©1992 Instructional Fair, Inc.   55   IF0116 Spelling

Whispering Sounds

PUBLIC LIBRARY

Word List
whale when which
where why what whip
wheel while white

Use the Word List to unscramble the letters and write each word.

1. h p i w — whip
2. e h e w r — where
3. e w n h — when
4. l e h t w — white
5. h w i c h — which
6. w y h — why
7. h e w a l — whale
8. e l w h e — wheel
9. h t w a — what
10. w l h i e — while

©1992 Instructional Fair, Inc.   56   IF0116 Spelling

Use the Word List to write the words where they belong.

Words That Ask Questions
what   why
when   which
where

Use three of the words above to write questions. Be sure to end each sentence with a question mark.
Answers will vary.

Words That Name Things
whale   wheel   whip

Write the two words that do not belong in either category.
while   white

©1992 Instructional Fair, Inc.   57   IF0116 Spelling

These Tasty Treats

Word List
this   those
the   there
that   them
then   they
these   thing

Write the missing word in each sentence and circle the letters that make the /th/ sound.

1. We will go to the zoo with (th)em.
2. Sunday is (th)e first day of the week.
3. Nick will eat lunch. (Th)en he will go to the park.
4. She wants to play with (th)ese/(th)ose toys.
5. Please give (th)is note to your mother.
6. What is that (th)ing in the sky?
7. (Th)ere are two kittens in the basket.
8. Is (th)at your cat over there?
9. Are (th)ose/(th)ese gifts for Pat?
10. Will (th)ey go camping with us?

©1992 Instructional Fair, Inc.   58   IF0116 Spelling

Use the Word List to unscramble the letters and write the words. Then circle the letters that make the /th/ sound.

1. h t e s e — (th)ese
2. s t i h — (th)is
3. g h t i n — (th)ing
4. e h t — (th)e
5. t a h t — (th)at
6. o s h t e — (th)ose
7. n h e t — (th)en
8. y h t e — (th)ey
9. e t h r e — (th)ere
10. m h e t — (th)em

©1992 Instructional Fair, Inc.   59   IF0116 Spelling

Review

BLEND REVIEW

Pages 46-47 Match each blend to a group of letters to make a word.

fr —— ain   frog
tr —— og   train
gr —— and   grand
pr —— ive   prize
dr —— ize   drive
cr —— oss   cross

Pages 48-49 Write the word that names each picture.
glass   slide
flat   sleep
plane   fly

Pages 50-51 Read each clue. Unscramble the letters and write the word.

1. A slow animal (a i s n l) — snail
2. You put it on a letter. (a s m t p) — stamp
3. It is cold and white. (n o s w) — snow
4. To turn around (s n p i) — spin
5. You cook on it. (t o s v e) — stove
6. Your nose does this. (l m e s l) — smell

©1992 Instructional Fair, Inc.   60   IF0116 Spelling

Pages 52-55 Circle the misspelled word in each sentence. Write the word correctly on the line.

1. He fell and bumped his (chin). — chin
2. My (shoo) is too little. — shoe
3. A (chark) has sharp teeth. — shark
4. We will sail on a (chip). — ship
5. The (shildrin) play in the park. — children
6. Dave will (shop) the logs. — chop

Pages 56-59 Add th or wh to the groups of letters and write the missing words.

th em y ing eel at wh

Ex. That is an odd-looking th + ing.

1. Why is Bob late?
2. What time is it?
3. Where is that can of paint?
4. The wheel on the cart broke.
5. I saw them go home.

©1992 Instructional Fair, Inc.   61   IF0116 Spelling

Colorful Celebration

black purple brown
yellow orange red
white green pink blue

Match each color to a sentence and write the missing word.

1. Strawberry yogurt is pink
2. Snow is very white
3. A pumpkin is orange
4. The sky is often blue
5. Mud is brown
6. Ripe tomatoes are red
7. A panda bear is white and black
8. Grass is green
9. Plums are purple
10. Lemons are yellow

Which color is your favorite? Answers will vary.

©1992 Instructional Fair, Inc.   62   IF0116 Spelling

©1992 Instructional Fair, Inc.   IF0116 Answer Key

Use the code to color the picture.

1	red
2	yellow
3	blue
4	green
5	orange
6	purple
7	brown
8	white
9	black
10	pink

Use the picture to write the missing color words on the lines.

The boy with the **black** hair is wearing a **yellow** shirt and **blue** shorts. The girl with the **brown** hair is wearing a **red** shirt and **white** shorts. They like to lick the **pink** strawberry ice-cream cones. Oops! The **orange** balloon got away. But the boy still has his **purple** balloon and the girl still has her **green** balloon.

If you had a balloon, what color would it be? **Answers** What color is your favorite ice-cream flavor? **will vary.**

©1992 Instructional Fair, Inc.   63   IF0116 Spelling

When It Counts!

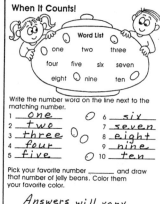

Word List

one   two   three
four   five   six   seven
eight   nine   ten

Write the number word on the line next to the matching number.

1	**one**	6	**six**
2	**two**	7	**seven**
3	**three**	8	**eight**
4	**four**	9	**nine**
5	**five**	10	**ten**

Pick your favorite number _____ and draw that number of jelly beans. Color them your favorite color.

Answers will vary.

Write the number word that tells how many jelly beans you drew. **Number must agree with number of beans drawn.**

©1992 Instructional Fair, Inc.   64   #0116 Spelling

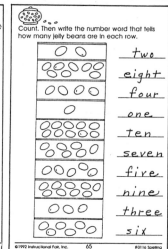

Count. Then write the number word that tells how many jelly beans are in each row.

	two
	eight
	four
	one
	ten
	seven
	five
	nine
	three
	six

©1992 Instructional Fair, Inc.   65   #0116 Spelling

Order Here!

SUPER BURGERS

Word List

first   next   last
after   before   left
right   here   there   now

Use the Word List and write each word that means the opposite.

first	*last*
before	*after*
right	*left*
there	*here*
after	*before*
here	*there*
left	*right*
last	*first*

Which two words are not opposites?
next   *now*

©1992 Instructional Fair, Inc.   66   IF0116 Spelling

Look carefully at the pictures. Then use the Word List to write the missing words on the lines.

FINISH LINE   TROPHY

1. The girl is standing to the **right** of the trophy.
2. The rabbit crosses the finish line **first**.
3. The cat crosses the finish line **next**.
4. The dog will cross the finish line **last**.
5. The boy is standing to the **left** of the trophy.
6. The cat will cross the line **before** the dog.
7. The dog will cross the line **after** the cat.

FINISH LINE

Write the three words not used in the sentences.
here   *there*   *now*

©1992 Instructional Fair, Inc.   67   #0116 Spelling

Sightseeing

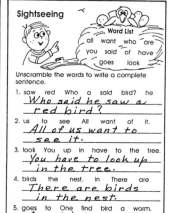

Word List

all   want   who   are
you   said   of   have
goes   look

Unscramble the words to write a complete sentence.

1. saw   red   Who   a   said   bird?   he
   Who said he saw a red bird?

2. us   to   see   All   want   of   it.
   All of us want to see it.

3. look   You   up   in   have   to   the   tree.
   You have to look up in the tree.

4. birds   the   nest.   In   There   are
   There are birds in the nest.

5. goes   to   One   find   bird   a   worm.
   One bird goes to find a worm.

©1992 Instructional Fair, Inc.   68   #0116 Spelling

Read each sentence. Use the Word List to write the missing word in the boxes.

1. _____ are a good friend.   **you**

2. They _____ it was fun.   **said**

3. Matt _____ to camp.   **goes**

4. Do you know _____ lives there?   **who**

5. Please _____ for the book.   **look**

6. Ted and Jenny _____ to read.   **want**

7. They _____ going swimming.   **are**

8. Do you _____ a pet?   **have**

9. They saw a litter _____ pups.   **of**

10. Amy picked _____ of the flowers.   **all**

©1992 Instructional Fair, Inc.   69   #0116 Spelling

Review

Pages 62-63 Write the correct color word.
1. A flamingo is **pink**   6. A plum is **purple**
2. The sea is **blue**   7. Mud is **brown**
3. A banana is **yellow**   8. A 🍎 is **red**
4. An 🟠 is **orange**   9. A leaf is **green**
5. A 🐧 is **black** and **white**.

Pages 64-65 Count the objects and write the correct number word on the line next to each picture.

🐚 *three*	⚾ *nine*
⚽ *one*	🍪 *ten*
🔑 *six*	🦴 *eight*
⛸ *seven*	🥄 *four*
🎀 *two*	🧤 *five*

©1992 Instructional Fair, Inc.   70   #0116 Spelling

Pages 66-69 Read each sentence. Circle the missing word that is spelled correctly and write it on the line.

1. He will read the book **first** (ferst / (first))
2. That is the **last** cupcake. (lest / (last))
3. I will play **after** I do my work. (affer / (after))
4. We can eat lunch **before** we go. (befour / (before))
5. They must catch the bus **now** (here / (now))
6. The car will turn to the **right** (rit / (right))
7. Please bring the book **here**. (here / her)
8. Robin and Joe **want** to see the kittens. ((want) / wont)
9. She **said** it was a very old ship. ((said) / sed)
10. All **of** the children will go to the zoo. ((of) / uv)
11. Evan and Jill **have** new skates. ((have) / hav)
12. There **are** five frogs in the pond. ((are) / ar)
13. David **goes** fishing every day. (gos / (goes))
14. **Who** is your new friend? (whoo / (who))

©1992 Instructional Fair, Inc.   71   #0116 Spelling

©1992 Instructional Fair, Inc.   IF0116 Answer Key

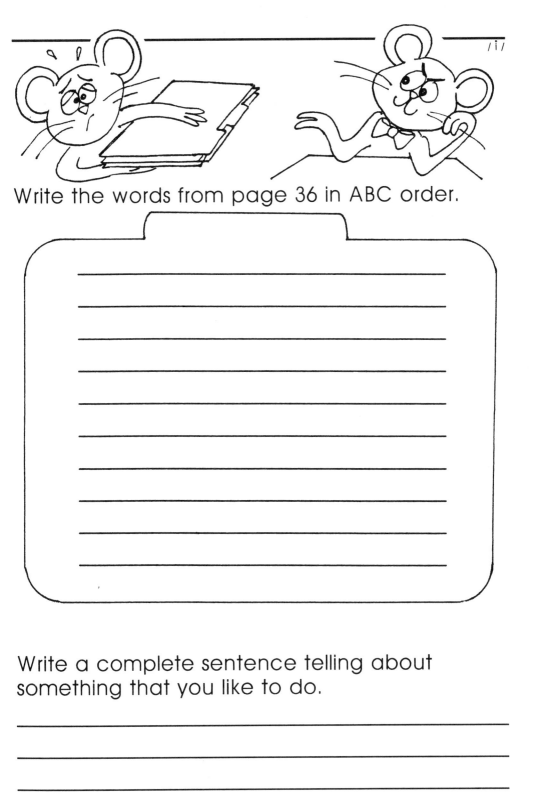

Write the words from page 36 in ABC order.

Write a complete sentence telling about something that you like to do.

Eyeing the Sky

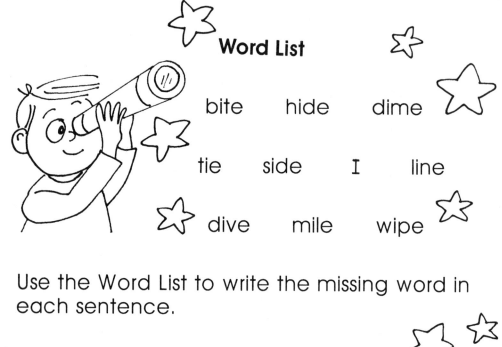

Word List

bite   hide   dime

tie   side   I   line

dive   mile   wipe

Use the Word List to write the missing word in each sentence.

1. The gum costs a _____.
2. Write your name on the _____.
3. The puppy will _____ the bone.
4. Please _____ the dishes.
5. Can you run a _____?
6. My mom and _____ like to read.
7. The duck will _____ into the pond.
8. You must play on this _____ of the street.
9. Mike will put on a _____.
10. Where did she _____ the gift?

Use the Word List to circle the hidden words.
Then write each word on the line.

1. crumbite   _____

2. aIerald   _____

3. snhideish   _____

4. fsideels   _____

5. btiend   _____

6. golineds   _____

7. skwipet   _____

8. wmilels   _____

9. sdimehap   _____

10. mesdivec   _____

Choose two words from the Word List and write
them in a sentence.

_____

_____

Motoring Home

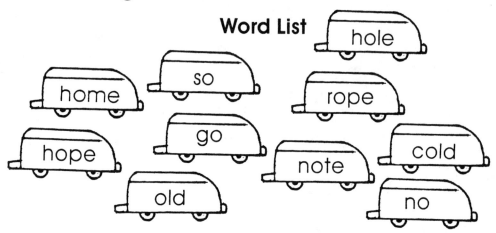

Word List

home · so · hole · rope · go · hope · note · cold · old · no

Write the words that rhyme with each picture.

_____   _____

_____

_____

_____

_____

Which word did not rhyme
with any of the pictures?

_____

Draw a picture of your home.

Read the clues. Use the
Word List to complete
the puzzle.

Across
2. A short letter
4. Not young
5. Where you live
6. Thick string

Down
1. Not hot
3. You can
   dig one
5. Wish for

Write the three words that are not in the puzzle.

_____ _____ _____

Write your home address.

_____

_____

_____

Go for the Goal

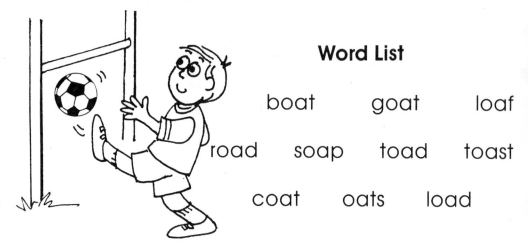

Word List

boat goat loaf

road soap toad toast

coat oats load

Read the clues. Write the correct word(s).

1. It begins like 🍃 _____ _____

2. It begins like ⚪ _____

3. It begins like 🐱 _____

4. It begins like 🧣 _____

5. It begins like ⚾ _____

6. It begins like GUM _____

7. It begins like 🐰 _____

8. It begins like 2 _____ _____

What two letters are the same in every word?

_____

Use the Word List to complete the puzzle.

Across

3. A farm animal

4. You use bread to make this.

6. A horse eats this.

8. To fill a truck

9. A street

Down

1. It sails.

2. You wear it.

5. It lives in a pond.

7. You use it to wash.

8. You buy a ____ of bread.

Review

Pages 28-31 Write the / ā / word that names each picture.

1. _____

2. _____

3. _____

4. _____

5. _____

6. _____

7. _____

8. _____

Pages 32-35 Use the code to write the missing / ē / word in each sentence.

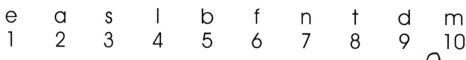

e	a	s	l	b	f	n	t	d	m
1	2	3	4	5	6	7	8	9	10

1. A __ __ __ __ lives in the sea.
  3 1 2 4

2. The __ __ __ buzzed around the flower.
  5 1 1

3. How do you __ __ __ __ ?
  6 1 1 4

4. He keeps his room very __ __ __ __ .
  7 1 2 8

5. We planted a __ __ __ __ .
  3 1 1 9

6. Do you like to eat __ __ __ __ ?
  10 1 2 8

7. Will you come to the park with __ __ ?
  10 1

8. The __ __ __ __ fell off the tree.
  4 1 2 6

Pages 36-39 Unscramble the letters and write the missing / ī / word in each sentence.

1. This shirt is just the right _____. (zise)

2. Let's take a _____ up the hill. (kehi)

3. Did you fly your _____ yesterday? (ikte)

4. Mike likes to _____ into the pool. (vide)

5. That dog does not _____. (ibte)

6. Can we _____ on the train? (ierd)

7. This balloon costs a _____. (mdie)

8. Please help me _____ the ribbon. (ite)

Pages 40-43 Circle the misspelled words. Then write them correctly on the lines.

Bob and I wanted to ho fishing. I put on my warm kote. Bob helped me foad the boat. We drove down the ood rood. We untied the rowp and slid the boot into the lake. It was zo kold that we gave up and went tome.

_____   _____

_____   _____

_____   _____

_____   _____

_____   _____

Grab Bag

Word List

free	cross	grand
grass	grade	train	prize
from	drive	frog

Write the missing words on the lines. Use the numbered letters to solve the code.

1. He will win first _ _ _ _ _ _.

       1

2. Can you _ _ _ _ _ a car?

       2

3. It was a _ _ _ _ _ parade.

     3

4. Be careful when you _ _ _ _ _ the road.

       4

5. What _ _ _ _ _ will you be in next year?

     5

6. We will ride the _ _ _ _ _ to the city.

     6

7. The _ _ _ _ hopped into the pond.

   7

8. Brenda likes to cut the _ _ _ _ _.

     8

9. Brent got a new book _ _ _ _ his dad.

    9

10. They gave away _ _ _ _ balloons.

    10

Y _ _ u _ _ _ _
9   8   3   2

_ _ _ _ _ _ _ _!
6   5   10   10   1   7   1   4

IF0116 Spelling

Use the Word List to unscramble the letters inside each bag. Write the word correctly.

1. i r p z e _____

2. g d a r e _____

3. r e d v i _____

4. r e f e _____

5. r g s a s _____

6. t i r a n _____

7. o f r g _____

8. s c s o r _____

9. f o m r _____

10. d g a r n _____

Write a complete sentence to tell what you would like to find inside a bag.

_____

_____

Climbing High

Word List

class

plus   flat

glass   clap   slide

sleep   plan   fly   plane

Write the words that begin with
the same sound as _____. _____

_____

Write the words that begin with
the same sound as _____. _____

_____

Write the words that begin with the same sound
as _____.

_____   _____

Write the words that begin with the same sound
as _____.

_____

Write the word that begins with
the same sound as _____. _____

Don't get lost! Use the Word List to circle as many words as you can. Look → and ↓.

b	l	f	l	y	h	c	c	m	s	q
j	t	s	a	l	u	w	l	x	l	p
s	l	i	d	e	g	i	a	r	e	l
p	a	f	l	a	t	o	s	v	e	a
y	g	l	a	s	s	t	s	h	p	n
g	z	u	k	d	p	l	a	n	e	c

Write the words that you circled in the puzzle.

_____   _____

_____   _____

_____   _____

_____   _____

Write the two words that you did not find in the puzzle.

_____   _____

Squirrel-ly Skits

skate   snap   stove

spin   smile

smell   stamp   snow   stop   snail

Match each picture with a sentence and write the missing word.

1. Smiley Squirrel shovels the _____.

2. Squirt Squirrel can _____ the top.

3. Spot Squirrel likes to _____ in the mirror.

4. Stuper Squirrel will _____ the traffic for the _____.

5. Skipper Squirrel likes to _____ flowers.

6. Stray Squirrel put a pan on the _____.

7. Smokey Squirrel put a _____ on the letter.

8. Sprite Squirrel likes to _____ on the ice.

9. Scrappy Squirrel can _____ his fingers.

Unscramble the words to write a complete sentence.

1. can   flower.   The   smell   snail   the

_____

_____

2. on   skates?   Can   ice   you   spin

_____

_____

3. dropped   snow.   He   stamp   the   in   the

_____

_____

4. snapping   Please   your   stop   fingers.

_____

_____

5. cook   the   They   will   on   stove.

_____

_____

6. cheery   Everyone   smile.   a   loves

_____

_____

Chalk It Up

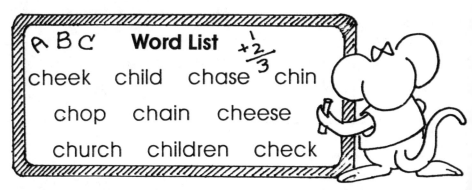

Word List

cheek   child   chase   chin

chop   chain   cheese

church   children   check

Write the word that names each picture.

1. _____

2. _____

3. _____

4. _____

5. _____

6. _____

7. _____

8. _____

9. _____

10. _____

Which word begins and ends with ch? _____

Use the Word List to write the words where they belong.

Body Parts

_____

_____

People

_____

_____

Things

Action Words

ABC

$\begin{array}{r} 1 \\ + 2 \\ \hline 3 \end{array}$

_____

_____

_____

_____

_____

_____

Use two of the action words in sentences.

_____

_____

_____

_____

_____

_____

Sharp Words

Word List

ship   shop   shape

shake   shut   shark   shell   sheep

she   shoe

Write the missing word in each sentence and circle the letters that make the /**sh**/ sound.

1. Shelly found a _____ in the sand.

2. A circle is a round _____.

3. The _____ hurts my foot.

4. We will sail on a _____.

5. _____ reads to her dad.

6. A _____ lives in the sea.

7. Please _____ the door.

8. The _____ ate the grass.

9. Please _____ the sand out of the blanket.

10. Do you like to _____ for new games?

Read each clue. Use the Word List to write the correct word on the lines. Then use the numbered letters to solve the code.

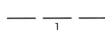

1. Opposite of he

___ ___ ___
    1

2. Another word for store

___ ___ ___ ___
        2

3. A turtle has one.

___ ___ ___ ___ ___
 3

4. Short, quick, movements

___ ___ ___ ___ ___
     4

5. A big fish

___ ___ ___ ___ ___
       5

6. A boat

___ ___ ___ ___
     6

7. You wear it on your foot.

___ ___ ___ ___
    7

8. A woolly animal

___ ___ ___ ___ ___
      8

9. A ▲ or a ■

___ ___ ___ ___ ___
    9

10. To close

___ ___ ___ ___ ___
     10

Y ___ ___ ___ ___ ___
  7 10   4 5 8

___ ___ ___ ___ ___ ___ ___ ___ ___ ___!
 3 10 6 8 5   3 1 9 5 2

Whispering Sounds

Word List

whale	when	which
where why	what	whip
wheel	while	white

Use the Word List to unscramble the letters and write each word.

1. h p i w   _____

2. e h e w r   _____

3. e w n h   _____

4. i e h t w   _____

5. h w i c h   _____

6. w y h   _____

7. h e w a l   _____

8. e l w h e   _____

9. h t w a   _____

10. w l h i e   _____

Use the Word List to write the words where they belong.

Words That Ask Questions

_____

_____

_____

Use three of the words above to write questions. Be sure to end each sentence with a question mark.

_____

_____

_____

_____

_____

_____

Words That Name Things

_____   _____   _____

Write the two words that do not belong in either category.

_____   _____

These Tasty Treats

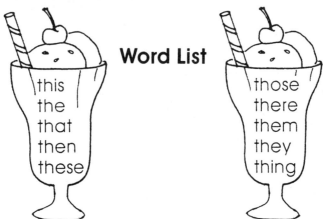

Word List

this
the
that
then
these

those
there
them
they
thing

Write the missing word in each sentence and circle the letters that make the /**th**/ sound.

1. We will go to the zoo with _____.

2. Sunday is _____ first day of the week.

3. Nick will eat lunch. _____ he will go to the park.

4. She wants to play with _____ toys.

5. Please give _____ note to your mother.

6. What is that _____ in the sky?

7. _____ are two kittens in the basket.

8. Is _____ your cat over there?

9. Are _____ gifts for Pat?

10. Will _____ go camping with us?

Use the Word List to unscramble the letters and write the words. Then circle the letters that make the /**th**/ sound.

1. h t e s e _____

2. s t i h _____

3. g h t i n _____

4. e h t _____

5. t a h t _____

6. o s h t e _____

7. n h e t _____

8. y h t e _____

9. e t h r e _____

0. m h e t _____

Review

Pages 46-47 Match each blend to a group of letters to make a word.

fr	ain	_____
tr	og	_____
gr	and	_____
pr	ive	_____
dr	ize	_____
cr	oss	_____

Pages 48-49 Write the word that names each picture.

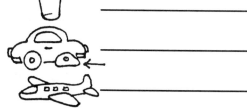

_____

_____

_____

_____

Pages 50-51 Read each clue. Unscramble the letters and write the word.

1. A slow animal (a i s n l) _____

2. You put it on a letter. (a s m t p) _____

3. It is cold and white. (n o s w) _____

4. To turn around (s n p i) _____

5. You cook on it. (t o s v e) _____

6. Your nose does this. (l m e s l) _____

Pages 52-55 Circle the misspelled word in each sentence. Write the word correctly on the line.

1. He fell and bumped his ckin. _____

2. My shoo is too little. _____

3. A chark has sharp teeth. _____

4. We will sail on a chip. _____

5. The shildrin play in the park. _____

6. Dave will shop the logs. _____

Pages 56-59 Add **th** or **wh** to the groups of letters and write the missing words.

| **th** | em | y | ing | eel | at | **wh** |

Ex. That is an odd-looking _th + ing_.

1. _____ is Bob late?

2. _____ time is it?

3. Where is _____ can of paint?

4. The _____ on the cart broke.

5. I saw _____ go home.

Colorful Celebration

black purple brown yellow orange red white blue green pink

Match each color to a sentence and write the missing word.

1. Strawberry yogurt is _____.

2. Snow is very _____.

3. A pumpkin is _____.

4. The sky is often _____.

5. Mud is _____.

6. Ripe tomatoes are _____.

7. A panda bear is white and _____.

8. Grass is _____.

9. Plums are _____.

10. Lemons are _____.

Which color is your favorite? _____

Use the code to color the picture.

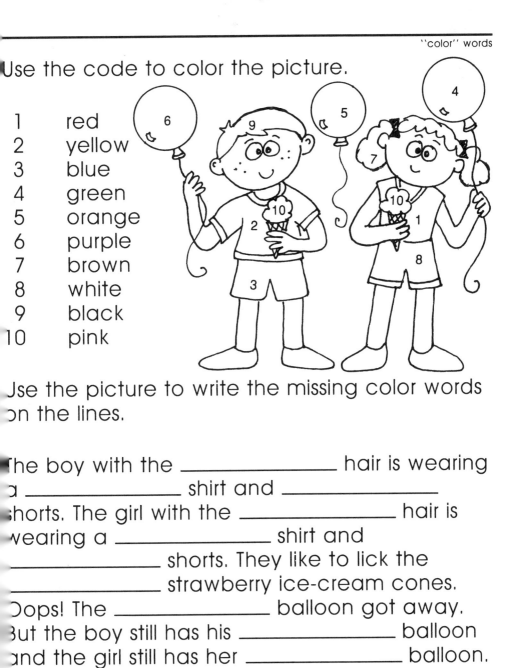

1 red
2 yellow
3 blue
4 green
5 orange
6 purple
7 brown
8 white
9 black
10 pink

Use the picture to write the missing color words on the lines.

The boy with the _____ hair is wearing a _____ shirt and _____ shorts. The girl with the _____ hair is wearing a _____ shirt and _____ shorts. They like to lick the _____ strawberry ice-cream cones. Oops! The _____ balloon got away. But the boy still has his _____ balloon and the girl still has her _____ balloon.

If you had a balloon, what color would it be? _____
What color is your favorite ice-cream flavor? _____

When It Counts!

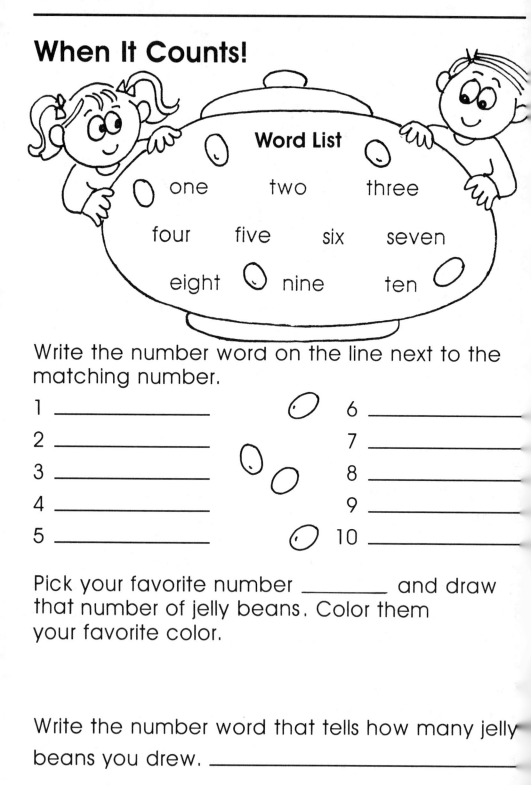

Word List

one	two	three
four	five	six	seven
eight	nine	ten

Write the number word on the line next to the matching number.

1 _____   6 _____

2 _____   7 _____

3 _____   8 _____

4 _____   9 _____

5 _____   10 _____

Pick your favorite number _____ and draw
that number of jelly beans. Color them
your favorite color.

Write the number word that tells how many jelly
beans you drew. _____

Count. Then write the number word that tells
how many jelly beans are in each row.

_____

_____

_____

_____

_____

_____

_____

_____

_____

_____

Order Here!

Use the Word List and write each word that means the opposite.

first   _____

before   _____

right   _____

there   _____

after   _____

here   _____

left   _____

last   _____

Which two words are not opposites?

_____   _____

Look carefully at the pictures. Then use the
Word List to write the missing words on the lines.

1. The girl is standing to the _____ of
   the trophy.

2. The rabbit crosses the finish line _____ .

3. The cat crosses the finish line _____ .

4. The dog will cross the finish line _____ .

5. The boy is standing to the _____ of
   the trophy.

6. The cat will cross the line _____ the
   dog.

7. The dog will cross the line _____ the
   cat.

Write the three words not used in the
sentences.

_____ _____ _____

Sightseeing

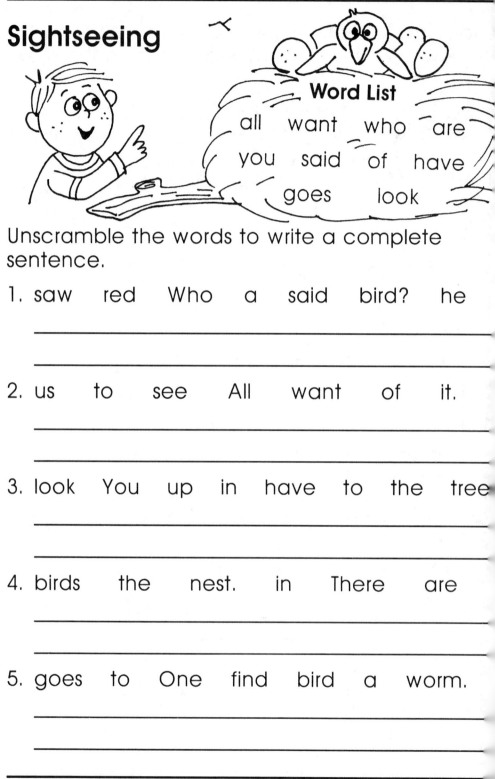

Word List

all	want	who	are
you	said	of	have
	goes	look	

Unscramble the words to write a complete sentence.

1. saw   red   Who   a   said   bird?   he

_____

_____

2. us   to   see   All   want   of   it.

_____

_____

3. look   You   up   in   have   to   the   tree

_____

_____

4. birds   the   nest.   in   There   are

_____

_____

5. goes   to   One   find   bird   a   worm.

_____

_____

Read each sentence. Use the Word List to write the missing word in the boxes.

1. ___ are a good friend.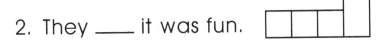

2. They ___ it was fun.

3. Matt ___ to camp.

4. Do you know ___ lives there?

5. Please ___ for the book.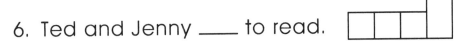

6. Ted and Jenny ___ to read.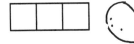

7. They ___ going swimming.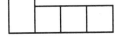

8. Do you ___ a pet?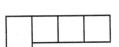

9. They saw a litter ___ pups.

10. Amy picked ___ of the flowers.

Review

Pages 62-63 Write the correct color word.

1. A flamingo is _____. 6. A plum is _____
2. The sea is _____. 7. Mud is _____
3. A banana is _____. 8. A 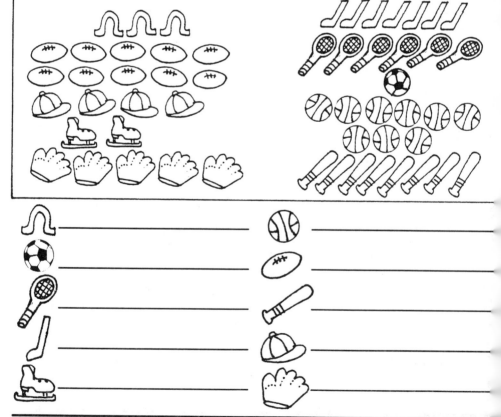 is _____
4. An ⚾ is _____. 9. A leaf is _____
5. A 🐧 is _____ and _____

Pages 64-65 Count the objects and write the correct number word on the line next to each picture.

Pages 66-69 Read each sentence. Circle the missing word that is spelled correctly and write t on the line.

1. He will read the book _____.
   ferst   first

2. That is the _____ cupcake.
   lest   last

3. I will play _____ I do my work.
   after   aftr

4. We can eat lunch _____ we go.
   befour   before

5. They must catch the bus _____.
   now   new

6. The car will turn to the _____.
   rit   right

7. Please bring the book _____.
   here   her

8. Robin and Joe _____ to see the kittens.
   want   wont

9. She _____ it was a very old ship.
   sed   said

0. All _____ the children will go to the zoo.
   uv   of

1. Evan and Jill _____ new skates.
   have   hav

2. There _____ five frogs in the pond.
   are   ar

3. David _____ fishing every day.
   gos   goes

4. _____ is your new friend?
   whoo   who